In the Beginning,
God created the heavens and the earth.
The Earth was dark and empty,
And the Spirit of God hovered over the waters.

The Beautiful Story
of the
Bible

The Beautiful Story of the Bible: Published 2015 by the Incorporated Catholic Truth Society, 40-46 Harleyford Road, London SE11 5AY. Tel: 020 7640 0042; Fax: 020 7640 0046; www.CTSbooks.org Copyright © 2015 The Incorporated Catholic Truth Society in this English-language edition.

ISBN: 978 1 78469 084 7   CTS Code CH63

Translated from the French Edition by Pierpaolo Finaldi: **La belle histoire de la Bible** written and illustrated by Maïte Roche, published 2009 by Edifa-Mame, 15-27 rue Moussorgski, 75018 Paris; ISBN Mame 978-2-7289-1282-7; Edifa 978-2-9163-5043-1; Copyright © Edifa Mame - 2009.

Maïte Roche

The Beautiful Story
of the
Bible

God said: "Let there be light!"

God said:
"Let the heavens be divided from the waters!"

od said: "Let the waters come together to make the sea, and let the continents appear. Let grass and plants spring up on the earth with their seeds inside and let the trees produce fruit each according to their different kind."

God said: "Let there be lights in the heavens to divide day from night and to mark out festivals, days and years."

od said: "Let the waters teem with living creatures, and let birds fly above the earth."

God said: "Let the earth produce every kind of living creature, cattle, reptiles and savage beasts."
God said: "Let us make man and woman in our own image".
God blessed them and said to them: "Be fruitful and multiply, fill the earth, I entrust it to you."
God saw that his creation was good.

God gave Adam and Eve a wonderful garden. He said to them: "You can eat of all the fruits in the garden except for the tree of the knowledge of good and evil, for if you do you will die."

But the serpent made Eve believe that the fruit would be good for her. Eve saw that the fruit was desirable, and she ate it and gave it to Adam. How unfortunate! They had disobeyed God, and had to leave that happy place. From that moment onwards their life would be difficult, but God would look after them and promised that one day, evil would be defeated.

There were now many people on the earth. but they made war against each other and their hearts were full of wickedness. God wanted to save his creation from evil and to make everything new again. Only Noah was a good and faithful man so God said to him: "Build an ark for yourself and your family and for two animals of each species for I am going to send a great flood." Noah obeyed and did what God told him.

*I*t rained and rained for forty days and forty nights, it was a great flood! The waters covered the whole earth.

Only Noah's ark remained above the water. When the rain stopped, a dove flew from the ark and brought back an olive branch. This was the sign that life was returning to the earth. Noah and his family thanked God because he had saved them.

God blessed them and made a promise:

"The rainbow in the sky shall be the sign of my covenant of love with you for all time."

Abraham lived in a city called Ur of the
Chaldaeans. God said to him: "Leave your country
and go to the land that I will show you, I will make
of you a great nation." Abraham set out with Sarah his
wife, with his servants and all his animals.

He journeyed towards the country that God had promised him. God told him he would reward his faithfulness: "Abraham, look at the stars, your children's children will be as many as the stars in the heavens."

God brought Abraham to the promised land:
the land of Canaan. One day Abraham welcomed three
messengers from God. They announced to Abraham: 'In a
year's time, Sarah will have a son.' Sarah laughed because
she was too old to have a child! But nothing is impossible
for God, and sure enough a year later she brought a son
into the world. His name was Isaac. Abraham and Sarah
thanked God who had kept his promise.

saac married Rebecca and they had two sons who were twins; Esau, the eldest who was a great hunter and Jacob who was a shepherd. Isaac became very old and blind and wanted to bless his eldest son before he died. But Rebecca knew that God had chosen Jacob to receive the blessing from his father and that he would become the leader of the tribe instead of his brother. While Esau was hunting, she prepared a good soup. She dressed Jacob in one of Esau's tunics and covered his arms with fur so that he would be more like his brother.

That was how Jacob received the
blessing from Isaac. "May God give
you abundance, may the peoples serve you,
be the master of your brothers."

Jacob fled from his brother Esau's great anger. When night came, he fell asleep. In a dream he saw a ladder which reached from earth to heaven. On it, were angels going up and coming down.

God said to Jacob:
"I am the God of Abraham, of Isaac
and of Jacob. I will give you the land on
which you are lying, I will bless your
descendants, and will be with you
to guard you wherever you go."

God gave Jacob a new name: "Israel". Jacob had twelve sons, and together with their families they were all called the "children of Israel".

Jacob gave a beautiful tunic to Joseph his
favourite son. His brothers were jealous and plotted
against him. When Joseph went to join his brothers
in the fields, they took his beautiful tunic. They
sold him as a slave for twenty pieces of silver to some
merchants who were on their way to Egypt. They
told Jacob that Joseph had been eaten by a wild
beast. Jacob was very sad.

n Egypt, God looked after Joseph and he became Pharaoh's prime minister thanks to his cleverness and his faithfulness. The harvests were very bad and there was a great famine in all the land. So Joseph allowed all his family to stay with him so that they would not die of hunger. When his brothers asked him for forgiveness, Joseph answered:

"God has turned the evil you did into good to save the lives of many people." Jacob felt such joy when he found his son Joseph again!

fter many years had passed, the children of Israel had grown to a great number in Egypt. They were known as the Hebrews. Their great number worried the Pharaoh for he wanted no one to be more powerful than him. So he made the Hebrews work as slaves to build his palaces and had all their newborn male babies thrown into the river.

One mother put her son in a basket and hid him among the reeds so that he would live. Miriam, his sister watched over the basket where the child lay.

When Pharaoh's daughter came to bathe in the river she was moved to discover the little baby and said:

"I will raise you as my own son, you will be called Moses for I saved you from the waters." Pharaoh's daughter asked Miriam: "Do you know of a woman who can look after the child?" Miriam went quickly to find her mother who was full of joy because her son had been saved!

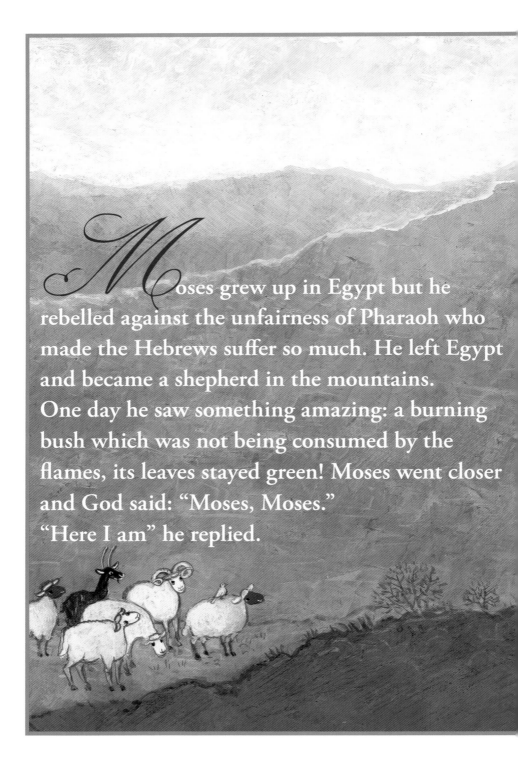

*M*oses grew up in Egypt but he rebelled against the unfairness of Pharaoh who made the Hebrews suffer so much. He left Egypt and became a shepherd in the mountains.
One day he saw something amazing: a burning bush which was not being consumed by the flames, its leaves stayed green! Moses went closer and God said: "Moses, Moses."
"Here I am" he replied.

God said: "I am the God of Abraham, of Isaac and of Jacob, I have seen the suffering of my people in the land of Egypt, go and free them, I will be with you."
Moses asked: "What is your name?"
God answered: "I am he who is."

oses and his brother Aaron went to see Pharaoh. "This is what our God has said: 'Let my people go!'" But Pharaoh's heart was hard and he answered: "I will not allow it, I do not know your God!"

So God sent plagues upon all of Egypt until
Pharaoh saw his power and let the Hebrews go.

God said to Moses: "You shall prepare a meal and you shall eat it in haste, for tonight you will be freed from slavery." It was the feast of Passover, celebrating the passage of the Lord. That very night after the last plague, Pharaoh finally let the Hebrews go and a great multitude began the long march to the promised land.

haraoh soon regretted
letting the Hebrews go. He hurried
after them with his armies. The Hebrews
were terrified, the sea was in front of them and they
could not move forward. So God said to Moses:
"Raise your staff, and hold out your hand over the
sea and divide it in two." Moses obeyed God and the

people crossed the sea on dry land. Then the sea closed again on Pharaoh and his army. The people sang and danced, thanking God who had freed them!

In the desert the Hebrews began to complain, they were hungry and thirsty and they grumbled against Moses.

So God said to Moses: "Strike the rock with your staff, water will gush out and the people will drink. I will make bread come down from heaven. Each morning you will gather your daily bread."

Every morning the manna fell like dew on the earth and the people collected the small white seeds which tasted like honey cake.

"I am your God, and there is no other. You will love me with all your heart."

On the mountain God gave
Moses the Ten Commandments
to teach people to be faithful to God and live in peace
with each other by doing what is right.
The Word of God was inscribed on two stone tablets:
these were the tablets of the Law which Moses brought
to the people. They were placed in a beautiful box called
the Ark of the Covenant which was kept inside a tent.
So the Word of God stayed in the midst of his people.

he Hebrews could not enter the land of
Canaan because their enemies were protected by the
great fortress of Jericho. So God said to Joshua: "Take
the Ark of the Covenant around the walls of the city
every day for seven days.

On the seventh day blow the trumpets and raise a great war cry. Then the walls of the city will crumble and I will give you victory."
After forty years in the desert the people of Israel finally entered the promised land.

The descendants of the twelve sons of Jacob became the twelve tribes of Israel. They lived together in the land of Canaan which they had conquered.

Ruth was a foreigner from Moab, but she said
to her old mother in law Naomi: "Wherever you
go, I will go, your people shall be my people and
your God will be my God." The two women
set out for the little village of Bethlehem. They
were very poor so Ruth went into the fields to
collect the wheat left behind by the farmers
to make some bread. Boaz was touched by her
faithfulness and asked to marry her. Ruth would
become the grandmother of King David.

Samuel served God in the temple at Shiloh. One night, God called him: "Here I am", answered Samuel. He ran to the old priest Eli thinking that he had called him. But it was not Eli.

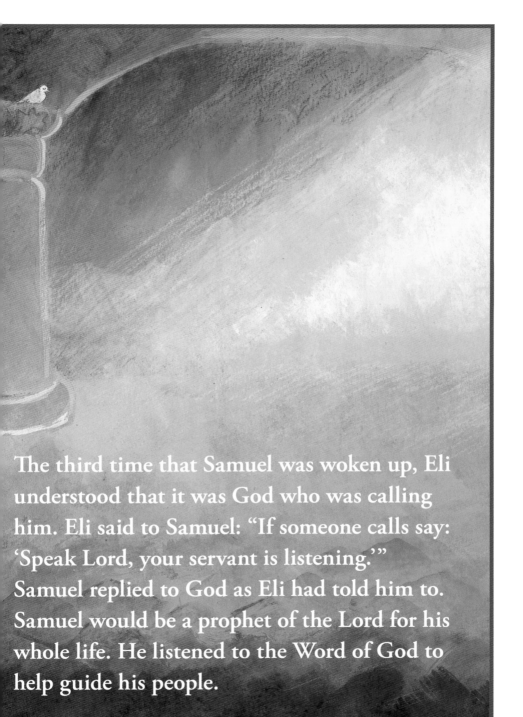

The third time that Samuel was woken up, Eli understood that it was God who was calling him. Eli said to Samuel: "If someone calls say: 'Speak Lord, your servant is listening.'"
Samuel replied to God as Eli had told him to. Samuel would be a prophet of the Lord for his whole life. He listened to the Word of God to help guide his people.

The people went to Samuel and asked him to choose a king to lead the country. God said to Samuel: "Go to Bethlehem to the family of Jesse, you will anoint the one that I will show you."

Of all the eight sons of Jesse, God did not pick the oldest or the strongest, for he looks at the heart. He chose David, the youngest who was a shepherd.

David was anointed and from that day onwards, the Spirit of the Lord was with him. As he looked after his sheep, David played the harp and sang to God: "The Lord is my shepherd, there is nothing I shall want".

ar broke out with the Philistines. Goliath the
giant challenged the armies of Israel: "If anyone dares to
fight against me, the winner shall win the war!" Only
David was brave enough to answer Goliath's challenge.
So he went to fight the giant with his sling and five
smooth stones he had collected from the stream.

Goliath laughed at him and mocked him.

David said: "You come against me with a sword and a spear, but I come against you in the name of the Lord and it is he who gives victory!" David took out his sling and threw a stone which hit Goliath in the forehead. Goliath fell face down into the dust. Everyone saw that it is God who gives victory to his people.

avid became king and led the Ark of the Covenant into Jerusalem, they went in procession, singing for joy. The king was dressed in a simple linen cloth and he danced in front of the ark. "All people clap your hands, acclaim the Lord with shouts of joy!"

King Solomon continued the work of his father, King David. God blessed him with great wisdom. He built a magnificent temple and called together the people for a great feast to accompany the Ark of the Covenant which was put in a sacred place called the Holy of Holies. The Ark was brought in procession to the temple and the smoke of the offerings and the incense rose to God. Solomon blessed the people and made this prayer:

"Lord, listen to the prayers of everyone who prays in this temple and forgive those who turn their hearts toward you."

The people forgot the love of God. Wars with neighbouring countries brought great suffering and destruction. God called prophets to be his messengers and to remind the people of his love and to give them hope.

God said: "Who will be my messenger?" Isaiah answered: "I am here, send me!" And he proclaimed to everyone: "Listen to your God, do not do evil, be good to one another, learn to do good. A great light will shine on those who walk in darkness, God himself will come to save you. A child will be born, the Spirit of the Lord will be upon him, He will bring peace and joy."

God sent the Angel Gabriel
to announce some wonderful news
to Mary, a young girl from Galilee.

He went into her house and said to her:
"Hail, Mary, full of grace, the Lord is with you.
God has chosen you to be the mother of his Son,
Jesus, the Saviour; the Holy Spirit will come
upon you." Mary accepted. She said:
"I am the handmaid of the Lord."

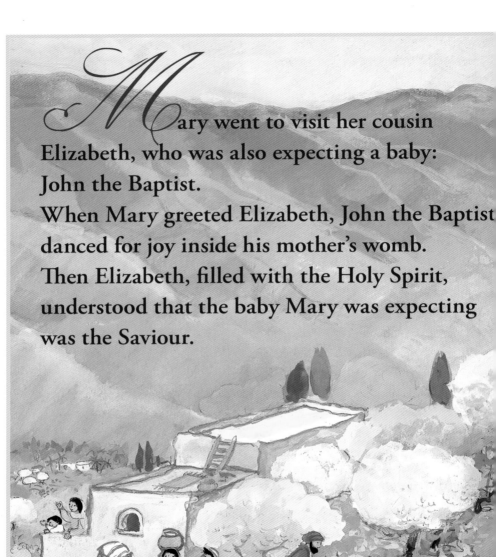

ary went to visit her cousin
Elizabeth, who was also expecting a baby:
John the Baptist.
When Mary greeted Elizabeth, John the Baptist
danced for joy inside his mother's womb.
Then Elizabeth, filled with the Holy Spirit,
understood that the baby Mary was expecting
was the Saviour.

She cried out: "Mary, you are blessed among women, and your child is blessed!"
Mary replied joyfully:
"God has done marvels for me!"

On the day of the wedding of Joseph and Mary, there was a big celebration in Nazareth. Joseph knew that Mary was expecting Jesus, the Son of God. He was going to love and protect Jesus like a father.

Jesus was born in Bethlehem.
He was laid in a manger.
Glory to God, and peace on earth!

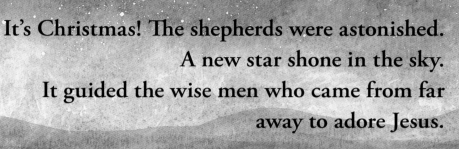

It's Christmas! The shepherds were astonished.
A new star shone in the sky.
It guided the wise men who came from far
away to adore Jesus.

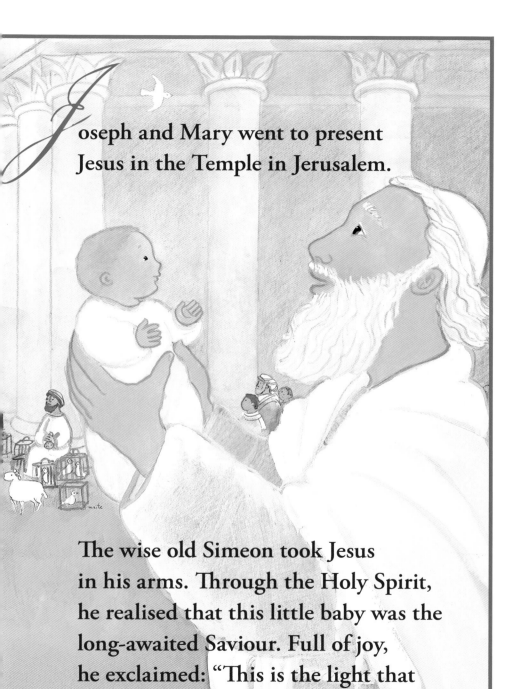

*J*oseph and Mary went to present Jesus in the Temple in Jerusalem.

The wise old Simeon took Jesus in his arms. Through the Holy Spirit, he realised that this little baby was the long-awaited Saviour. Full of joy, he exclaimed: "This is the light that will enlighten all nations!"

hen Jesus was twelve, he stayed for three days in the Temple in Jerusalem with the wise men and priests. They were completely amazed at his intelligence and how he understood the word of God.

Joseph and Mary were very worried, and searched for him high and low. When they found him again, Jesus said to them:

"Why were you searching for me? My Father's house is where I have to be."

ohn the Baptist grew up. He announced to everyone that the Saviour was coming: "Be converted, prepare your hearts, for the Lord is coming."

And he baptised them in the water of the
River Jordan. When Jesus was baptised,
the Holy Spirit came down on him like a dove,
and a voice was heard saying: "This is my
beloved Son, with whom I am well pleased."

eter and his brother Andrew, James and his brother John, were fishing on the lake. Jesus called them and said to them: "Come, follow me, I will make you into fishers of men." They left everything and followed him. Jesus also called Philip, Bartholomew, Thomas and Matthew, James the son of Alphaeus, Thaddaeus, Simon and Judas. These were the twelve Apostles.

A great crowd came up the mountain to listen to Jesus. He announced the Good News for everyone: "Rejoice, the Kingdom of God is a Kingdom of love, where you will be happy forever. God welcomes the poor and comforts those who are crying. Happy are the meek, they will possess the promised land."

"Happy are those who forgive,
they will be forgiven. Happy are
the peacemakers, they will be
called God's children."

A disciple asked Jesus: "Lord, teach us how to pray." Jesus replied,

"When you pray, say:
Our Father, who art in Heaven,
hallowed be thy name.
Thy kingdom come,
thy will be done on earth as it is in Heaven.
Give us this day our daily bread,
and forgive us our trespasses, as we forgive those who trespass against us, and lead us not into temptation, but deliver us from evil."

Lots of sick people came to Jesus, and he cured them: now the blind can see, the deaf can hear, the lame can walk again. One day, a paralysed man was even lowered through the roof of the house!

Jesus said to him: "I forgive you your sins. Get up, pick up your stretcher and go back home!" The paralysed man got up at once – he was cured! Lots of people started wondering: "Who is Jesus? He does things that only God can do!"

huge crowd followed Jesus up the mountainside. It was evening, people were hungry, and they had nothing to eat. A boy brought five loaves of bread and two fish to Jesus: It was very little for so many people!

Jesus took the loaves, blessed them and broke them up, then he gave them out. He did the same with the fishes. After the meal, there were twelve basketfuls of leftovers. Everyone had enough to eat, and went home rejoicing.

*J*esus crossed the lake with his disciples.
A violent storm broke out,
and the disciples were terrified.
"Help, Lord, save us!" Then Jesus said:
"Why are you afraid, men of little faith!"
He rebuked the wind and said to the sea:
"Silence! Be quiet!" and everything
became calm. The disciples asked each other:
"But who is he? Even the wind
and the sea obey him!"

The disciples wanted to stop some children from coming to Jesus. Jesus didn't agree: "Let the little children come to me, the Kingdom of God belongs to them, and to people who are like them."

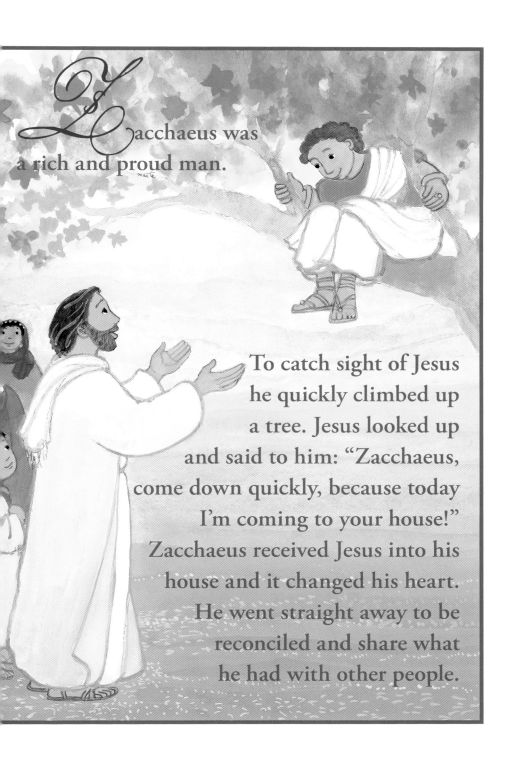

Zacchaeus was a rich and proud man.

To catch sight of Jesus he quickly climbed up a tree. Jesus looked up and said to him: "Zacchaeus, come down quickly, because today I'm coming to your house!" Zacchaeus received Jesus into his house and it changed his heart. He went straight away to be reconciled and share what he had with other people.

Jesus arrived in Jerusalem with his friends. He was hailed as a king: lots of people spread their cloaks on the road, others waved palm-branches and sang:

"Hosanna! Hosanna! Blessed is he who comes in the name of the Lord!"

*J*esus was teaching in the Temple. A scribe asked him: "Which Commandment is the greatest?" Jesus answered: "Love the Lord your God with all your heart, and your neighbour as yourself." But the leaders of the Temple had hard hearts. They wouldn't listen to Jesus, and they didn't believe that he was the Son of God. They wanted to arrest him and put him to death, but they were afraid of the crowd that surrounded him. In secret, they promised Judas thirty pieces of silver to help them arrest Jesus when he was alone.

Jesus knew that Judas was going to betray him, and that he was going to die.

He gathered his Apostles together for a last meal. He wanted to prepare their hearts for all that was going to happen.

He knelt before Peter to wash his feet.
Peter refused to let Jesus, the Lord,
wash his feet like a servant. But Jesus insisted:
"Do what I do, serve one another and love
each other as I have loved you."

During the meal, Jesus took the bread and blessed it. He broke it and gave it to his friends, telling them: "This is my body, given up for you."

Then Jesus took the cup of wine, blessed it and gave it to them, saying: "This is my blood that will be poured out for everyone, for the forgiveness of sins to show my love forever."

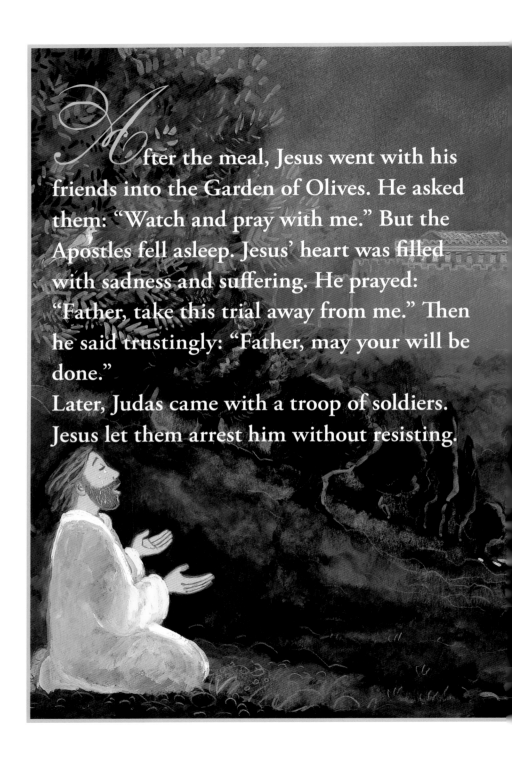

After the meal, Jesus went with his friends into the Garden of Olives. He asked them: "Watch and pray with me." But the Apostles fell asleep. Jesus' heart was filled with sadness and suffering. He prayed: "Father, take this trial away from me." Then he said trustingly: "Father, may your will be done."

Later, Judas came with a troop of soldiers. Jesus let them arrest him without resisting.

Almost all the Apostles ran away because they were afraid. Peter himself would say three times that he didn't know Jesus.

The leaders of the Temple asked Jesus:
"Are you the Son of God?"
"I am," replied Jesus.

Then they led Jesus to Pilate, the Roman ruler, to condemn him to death. The soldiers made fun of Jesus. They put a red cloak on him and a crown of thorns.

Pilate felt that Jesus shouldn't die, he had done nothing wrong. He said to the crowd: "Here is your king!" But they shouted: "Put him to death! Crucify him!" So Pilate let Jesus be condemned to death as a criminal.

Jesus went along the way
carrying a heavy cross.

He was exhausted. So the soldiers forced
Simon of Cyrene to help him. In the crowd,
Mary was filled with deep sorrow as she saw
her Son suffering so much. Beside her was
John, the faithful apostle, and some friends
who were crying.

The soldiers nailed Jesus to the cross with two criminals, and then shared out his clothes. The crowd made fun of him. Jesus said: "Father, forgive them, because they don't know what they're doing." Mary, John and some women were standing at the foot of the cross. Jesus entrusted John to Mary, saying: "This is your son," and he entrusted Mary to John, saying: "This is your mother." And he prayed: "Father, into your hands I commit my spirit." Then he died on the cross. A great darkness fell on the earth. Seeing all this, the centurion said: "Truly this man was the Son of God!" Evening came and they laid Jesus' body in a tomb, then they closed it with a large round stone.

On Easter Sunday, early in the morning, Mary Magdalen, Mary the mother of James, and Salome went to the tomb to embalm the body of Jesus with perfumes and spices. When they arrived, they saw that the entrance to the tomb was open!

An angel of the Lord spoke to them and said:
"Don't be afraid, Jesus is risen, he's not here
any more! Go and tell his disciples!"
Jesus is alive! Alleluia! Alleluia!
Jesus' friends were filled with joy.

*T*hat same evening, two disciples were walking to the village of Emmaus.

They were very sad because they did not yet know that Jesus had risen from the dead. Jesus began to walk with them but they didn't recognise him. As they walked he explained to them why the Christ had to give his life out of love so as to enter into God's glory. As they listened their hearts burned within them. When they arrived at Emmaus they invited Jesus to remain with them for it was nearly evening. During the meal, Jesus took the bread and said the blessing. He broke it and gave it to them. Then their eyes were opened and they recognised Jesus, but he disappeared.

They were full of joy and quickly got up and
ran back to Jerusalem to tell the Apostles what
had happened.
"We have seen the Lord, he is truly risen!"

eter, John, and some others had been fishing all night without catching any fish. In the morning, they found Jesus standing by the lakeside, he said to them:

"Throw the net to the right of the boat." Peter and his friends obeyed. They pulled in the net filled with big fishes. Then John recognised Jesus: "It is the Lord!"

Peter jumped straight into the water to go to
Jesus. Jesus prepared a meal with bread and fishes.
After the meal, he asked Peter three times:
"Do you love me?" Peter answered:
"Lord, you know everything, you
know that I love you." Then
Jesus chose him to guide all
those who believe in him: "You
will be the shepherd of my flock."

On the day of the Ascension, before
returning to God, his Father and our
Father, Jesus blessed his Apostles and
made them a promise:

"You are going to receive the strength of the Holy Spirit and you will be my witnesses to the ends of the earth." And Jesus went up to Heaven and disappeared from sight. Then they went back to Jerusalem and every day, they prayed together with one heart, filled with hope.

On the day of Pentecost, the Apostles were all gathered together. Suddenly there was a violent gust of wind, and something like flames of fire came and rested on them: they were filled with the Holy Spirit.

They went straight out into the streets to announce in every language the wonders that God had done.

eter spoke to the crowd with a loud voice: "Listen, all of you, Jesus worked signs and miracles among you, and yet you condemned him to die on a cross! But God has raised him from the dead and he is now seated at his right hand. Jesus received the Holy Spirit from his Father and gives it to us now."

They listened to the Word of God and welcomed it in their heart. Three thousand people were baptised that very day and received the Holy Spirit.

The new Christians listened to the Apostles speak about Jesus. They gathered in the temple and shared bread together in their houses as Jesus had commanded. They helped each other and shared everything they owned, praising God at all times.

As Peter went up to the Temple with John, he healed a lame man who began to jump for joy, praising God.

The chief priests in the temple had Peter and John thrown into prison and would let them go only if they stopped speaking about Jesus. But Peter and John answered: "We must listen to God and not to you, we cannot promise to stop proclaiming what we have seen and heard." The number of Christians increased day by day.

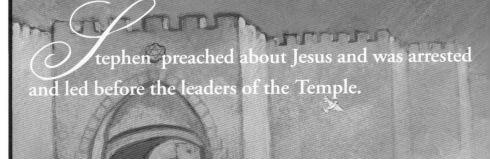

Stephen preached about Jesus and was arrested and led before the leaders of the Temple.

He was full of the Holy Spirit and his face was like that of an angel. He said to them: "I see the heavens open and Jesus sitting at the right hand of God." They could not accept these words so they dragged him outside the city and stoned him to death. They laid their cloaks at the feet of a man called Saul. Stephen died praying to God: "Lord Jesus, receive my spirit and forgive the evil they have done."

Saul was travelling to Damascus to arrest and imprison any Christians he could find. Suddenly a light from heaven shone all around him. He fell on the ground and heard a voice saying to him: "Saul, Saul, why are you persecuting me?" Saul asked: "Who are you, Lord?" "I am Jesus who you are persecuting." When Saul got up he had become blind. He remained blind for three days and was then baptised in the name of Jesus.

He was filled with the
Holy Spirit and regained his sight, he became
a disciple of Jesus and received a new name: Paul.

aul was completely changed by Jesus, he was even ready to give his life for him.

He went back to Jerusalem to speak to Peter and the Apostles who were very surprised by his conversion. Together they prayed to God to guide them. They understood that the Good News had to be proclaimed to all the peoples of the earth as Jesus had commanded: "Go and make disciples of all the nations." Paul was sent on a mission. He went to many countries to tell people about the risen Jesus and was accompanied by Barnabas then Titus, Silas and Timothy.

Paul, Peter, James and John wrote long letters to help the Christian communities live in unity in the Church which is the family of God. Paul wrote:

"Brothers, be joyful and live in peace.
May the grace of Jesus Christ,
the love of God and the communion
of the Holy Spirit be always with you."
We have been gathered together by the Holy
Spirit and called to enter with Jesus into the
Kingdom of God our Father.
"I am with you always, to the end of time."

CTS Children's Books

The Beautiful Story of Jesus, *by Maïte Roche* (CTS Code CH61)

The Bible for little children, *by Maïte Roche* (CTS Code CH60)

Getting to Know God, *by Christine Pedotti* (CTS Code CH9)

The Gospel for little children, *by Maïte Roche* (CTS Code CH1)

The Most Beautiful Christmas Story, *by Maïte Roche* (CTS Code CH8)

John Paul II, *by Elena Pascoletti* (CTS Code CH41)

Mother Teresa of Calcutta, *by Elena Pascoletti* (CTS Code CH45)

My Little Missal, *by Maïte Roche* (CTS Code CH20)

Prayers around the Crib, *by Juliette Levivier* (CTS Code CH7)

Praying at Mass, *by Juliette Levivier* (CTS Code CH11)

Praying with Mary, *by Juliette Levivier* (CTS Code CH62)

Praying with the Holy Spirit, *by Juliette Levivier* (CTS Code CH15)

The Rosary, *by Juliette Levivier* (CTS Code CH3)

Saint Anthony of Padua, *by Silvia Vecchini* (CTS Code CH16)

Saint Clare of Assisi, *by Francesca Fabris* (CTS Code CH46)

Saint Francis of Assisi, *by Silvia Vecchini* (CTS Code CH17)

Saint Joseph, *by Francesca Fabris* (CTS Code CH40)

Saint Lucy, *by Silvia Vecchini* (CTS Code CH19)

Saint Paul, *by Silvia Vecchini* (CTS Code CH22)

Saint Rita of Cascia, *by Silvia Vecchini* (CTS Code CH18)

Saint Thérèse of Lisieux, *by Silvia Vecchini* (CTS Code CH23)

The Way of the Cross, *by Juliette Levivier* (CTS Code CH4)

Why does Mary wear blue?, *by Pierpaolo Finaldi* (CTS Code CH4)